I am PERFECT just the way I am!

Copyright© 2020 Jennifer Abraham

All rights reserved. No part of this publication may be reproduced, stored in a retrieval system, or transmitted, in any form or by any means (electronic, mechanical, photocopying, recording, or otherwise), without the prior written permission of the publisher.

Thank you for buying an authorized edition of this book and for complying with copyright laws by not reproducing any part of it without permission. You are supporting writers and their hard work by doing this.

ISBN: 978-0-578-82029-3

Printed in the United States of America

10 9 8 7 6 5 4 3 2 1

For my PERFECTLY made children: Olivia, Aria and Alicia.

To my amazing husband, Sunil Abraham, who is my soulmate.

To my Father-In-Law, Thomas Abraham, who passed away from Creutzfeldt-Jakob Disease.

I hope to bring awareness to this monster disease.

I am PERFECT just the way I am!

The shape of my body is perfect!

No matter what other people say,

I am **PERFECT** just the way I am.

My name is
_____

and I am PERFECTLY made just the way I am.

About the Author

Jennifer Abraham has loved reading books all her life. She has been known to be stuck at the bus stop before school with a flashlight and book in hand. She wasn't always the coolest girl in school but always said that it doesn't matter what other people think about her. She is a Doctorate in Pharmacy and now lives in sunny Southern California. As a mother of 3 little princesses, she knows how important self confidence is. She loves to dance and sing, and is always having a dance party with her girls. Bollywood music is her favorite! She hopes this book introduces the positive effect of self-affirmation, and helps children build confidence and improve their academic performance and health.